The Greenwich Guide to

Day and

Night

Heinemann Library
Chicago, Illinois

Graham Dolan

Royal Observatory Greenwich

Published by Heinemann Library,
an imprint of Reed Educational & Professional Publishing,
Chicago, IL
Customer Service 888-454-2279

Visit our website at www.heinemannlibrary.com

Designed by Celia Floyd
Illustrations by Jeff Edwards
Originated by Dot Gradations
Printed in Hong Kong/China

05 04 03 02 01
10 9 8 7 6 5 4 3 2 1

Library of Congress Cataloging-in-Publication Data

Dolan, Graham, 1953-
  Day and night / Graham Dolan.
     p. cm. -- (The greenwich guide to)
Includes bibliographical references (p. 31) and index.
  ISBN 1-58810-042-1
  1. Earth--Rotation--Juvenile literature. 2. Day--Juvenile literature.
3. Night--Juvenile literature. [1. Earth--Rotation. 2. Day. 3. Night.]
I. Title.
  QB633 .D65 2001
  525'.35--dc21
                              00-010543

Acknowledgments
The publisher would like to thank the following for permission to reproduce photographs:
Francisco Diego, pp. 4, 6, 7, 18, 19, 21, 23 top, 27 top and bottom, 28, 29; NHPA, p. 11; Corbis, p. 13; National Maritime Museum, pp. 16, 17, 22, 23 bottom, 26.

Cover photograph reproduced with permission of Science Photo Library.

Spine logo reproduced with permission of the National Maritime Museum.

Every effort has been made to contact copyright holders of any material reproduced in this book. Any omissions will be rectified in subsequent printings if notice is given to the Publisher.

Some words are shown in bold, **like this.** You can find out what they mean by looking in the glossary.

Contents

Day and Night

The Sun is our nearest star. We can measure its size and its distance from us. We can see it, but cannot touch it or hear it. It gives us **energy**. Without it, there would be no life on Earth.

During the **day**, we receive light and heat from the Sun. This is when most people eat, drink, work, and play. At night, when it is dark, most of us go to bed and sleep. On clear nights, we can see stars, and sometimes the Moon and **planets,** too.

The stars and planets become visible at night.

Our spinning Earth

Our Earth is spinning on its **axis**. Half of Earth always points toward the Sun, and half always points away. When the part of Earth we are on faces the Sun, we receive light and energy. We call this **daytime**. As Earth spins, we eventually end up facing away from the Sun. When this happens, light and energy from the Sun can no longer reach us. It gets dark, and **nighttime** begins.

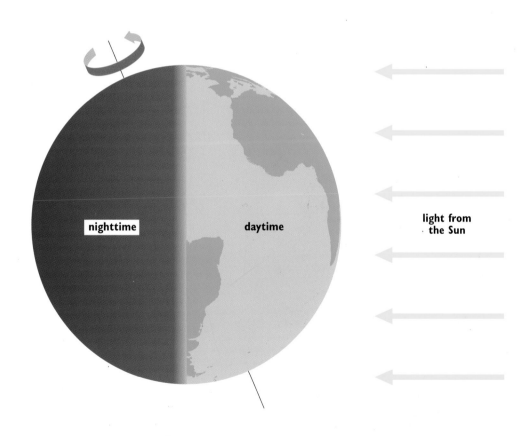

nighttime

daytime

light from the Sun

Earth spins on its axis once each day. The half facing the Sun is in daylight. The half facing away is in darkness.

The Sun

The Sun is just one of thousands of millions of stars that make up our **galaxy**, the Milky Way. It gives off light and **energy** that **radiate** out into space. The light and energy travel toward us at 186,000 miles (300,000 kilometers) a second. Traveling at this speed, it takes just over eight minutes to reach Earth's surface. The next closest star is Proxima Centauri, which is about 250,000 times farther away.

The temperature of the Sun

The Sun is a little like a giant nuclear power station. It produces huge amounts of energy every second. The inside is hotter than the outside. The **temperature** at its center is about 27 million °F (15 million °C). The temperature on the surface is about 9,900 °F (5,500 °C). Dark patches, called sunspots, are sometimes visible. The sunspots are regions of the Sun's surface that are cooler than the rest.

Never look directly at the Sun. It will damage your eyes. The dark spots you see here are called sunspots—each one is larger than Earth.

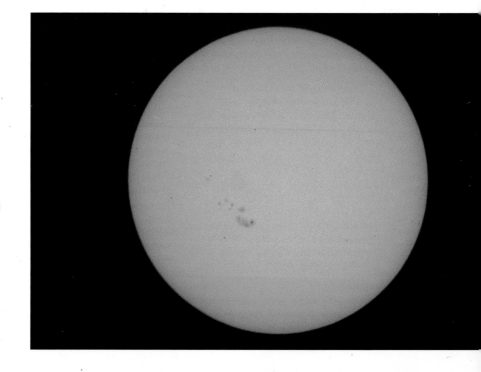

6

The Sun's brightness keeps us from seeing other stars during the day.

The size of the Sun

The Sun is about 100 times wider than Earth, and 400 times wider than the Moon. From Earth, the Sun and the Moon look about the same size in the sky. This is because the Sun is both 400 times wider than the Moon and also about 400 times farther away. The actual distance from Earth to the Sun is about 93 million miles (150 million kilometers).

The Sun's Path Across the Sky

The Sun, the Moon, and the stars appear to move across the sky in curved paths. This is because Earth is spinning on its **axis**.

The Sun's highest point

The Sun always rises over the **horizon** in the eastern half of the sky, and sets in the western half. It reaches its highest point at **midday**. It rises higher in the summer than it does in the winter. It rises and sets at a slightly different time, and in a slightly different direction, from one **day** to the next.

The area closest to the equator is called the Tropics.

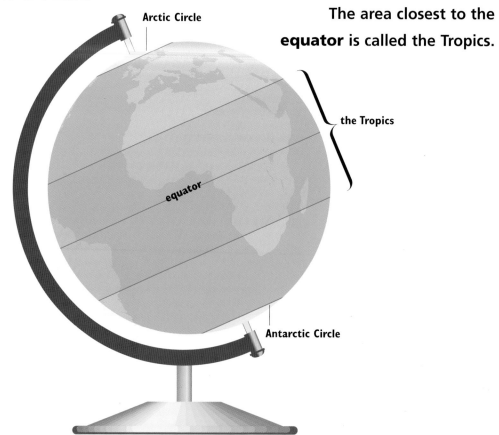

Arctic Circle

the Tropics

equator

Antarctic Circle

Clockwise or counterclockwise?

North of the Tropics, the midday Sun is always in the south. The Sun appears to move in a **clockwise** direction, from left to right.

South of the Tropics, the midday Sun is always in the north. The Sun appears to move in a **counterclockwise** direction, from right to left.

In the Tropics themselves, the midday Sun is sometimes in the north, and sometimes in the south, depending on the time of **year.**

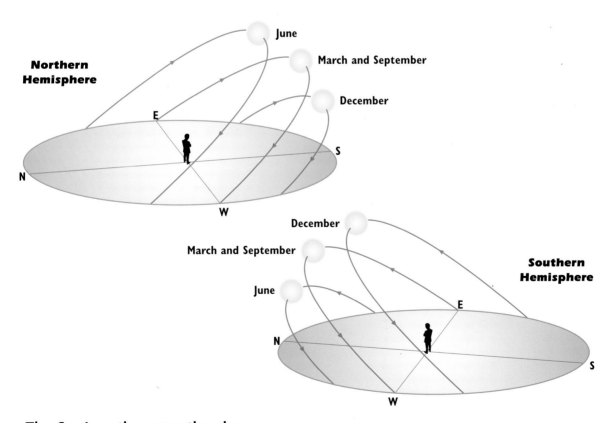

The Sun's path across the sky
changes throughout the year.

Day and Night in Different Places

In the summer, there are more hours of daylight each **day** than there are in the winter. This is because Earth leans as it **orbits** the Sun. In June, the North Pole leans toward the Sun. In December, it leans away from the Sun.

The poles—lands of midnight Sun

In June, places near the North Pole have 24 hours of daylight each day. In December, they have 24 hours of darkness. Near the South Pole, there are 24 hours of daylight each day in December, and 24 hours of darkness in June.

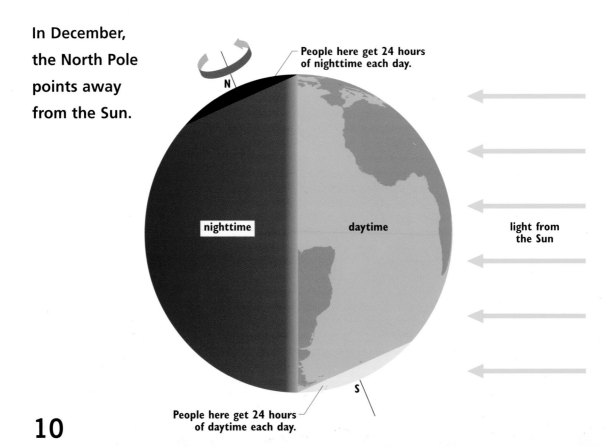

In December, the North Pole points away from the Sun.

People here get 24 hours of nighttime each day.

nighttime

daytime

light from the Sun

People here get 24 hours of daytime each day.

The Equator

Places along the **equator** get almost equal amounts of **daytime** and **nighttime** every day of the **year.** The farther north or south of the equator you go, the greater the difference between the amount of daytime you get each day in the summer and the winter.

This shows the Sun's path during a summer day near the North Pole.

midday

E

S

midnight

N

W

A time-lapse photo shows how the midsummer Sun at the North Pole reaches its lowest point at midnight, but does not actually set.

11

Shadows

When it is sunny, shadows are formed. Shadows can be used to figure out what time it is. They change in length and direction during the **day**.

Length and direction

The length of our shadows depends on the position of the Sun in the sky. As the Sun rises in the sky, the shadows get shorter and shorter. By **midday,** when the Sun is at its highest point, the shadows are at their shortest for that particular day. They then start to get longer again. They continue to grow in length until the Sun sets. The shadows always move in the same **clockwise** or **counterclockwise** direction as the Sun. The shadows at midday always fall along a north-south line.

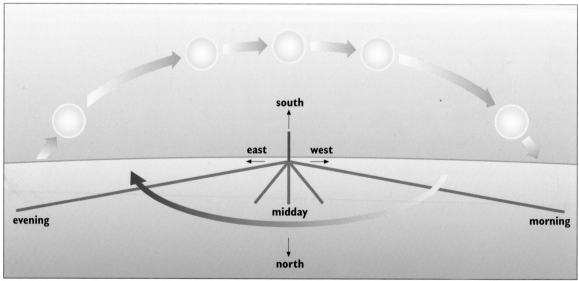

In the **Northern Hemisphere,** the Sun and shadows move in a clockwise direction. The midday Sun is always in the south.

Shadow sticks and sundials

Shadow sticks can be used to follow the path of the Sun across the sky. The shadow of a vertical stick is marked every half-hour with the help of a watch. Although the shadow of the stick always falls in a north-south direction at midday, the exact direction of the other shadows is different at different times of the year. As a result, shadow clocks made like this are not a very reliable way of finding out what the time is.

Sundials show the time more accurately. This is because the part that makes the shadow is specially angled. It is called a **gnomon**.

The time shown on this sundial is about 3:30 P.M.

gnomon

Time Zones

Local time

The farther west you are, the later the Sun rises, and the later it sets. For example, when a **sundial** in London, England, says 12:00, one in Cardiff, Wales, to the west, will say only 11:48. The time shown by a sundial is called the **local time.** Until about 120 **years** ago, people usually set their clocks and watches to local time, using a sundial. Today, everyone in a particular country or **time zone** will set their clocks and watches to a standard time.

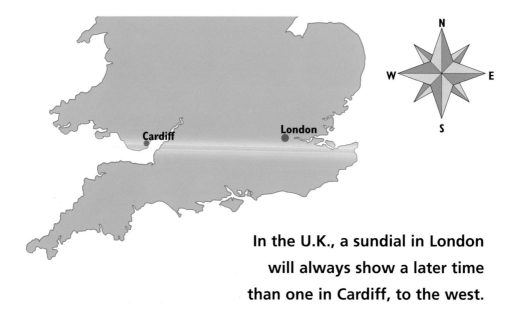

In the U.K., a sundial in London will always show a later time than one in Cardiff, to the west.

Daylight saving time

Some countries use **daylight saving time** for part of the year. Clocks are set forward one hour in the spring, and set back again in the autumn. The change allows people to make better use of the daylight hours in the summer.

Time zones

The world is divided into time zones. The time in each zone is usually one hour different from those on either side. In December, when it is 7:00 in the morning in New York, it is 10:00 in the morning in Rio de Janeiro, 12:00 noon in London, England, and 11:00 in the evening in Sydney, Australia.

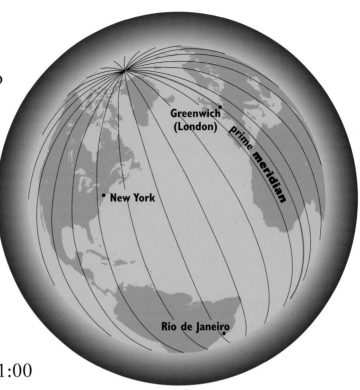

The world's countries fit loosely into a system of 24 time zones.

Some large countries, like the United States and Canada, are divided into several time zones. Others, such as China and India, use the same time for the whole country.

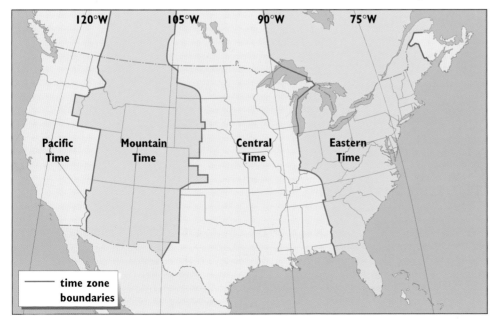

The United States and Canada have four main time zones.

A.M. and P.M.

The Sun at midday

At **midday,** the Sun passes from the eastern half of the sky to the western half. The imaginary line dividing the two halves is called a **meridian.** It runs in a north-south direction. When the Sun crosses the meridian, a nearby **sundial** will show 12:00. The Sun will have reached its highest point for the **day,** and shadows will be at their shortest.

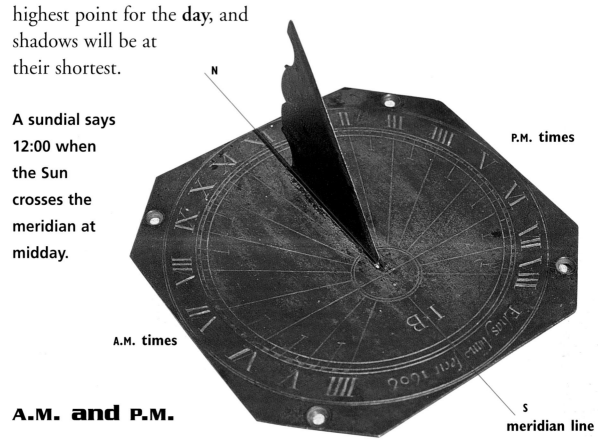

A sundial says 12:00 when the Sun crosses the meridian at midday.

N

P.M. times

A.M. times

S
meridian line

A.M. and P.M.

We often use the letters A.M. and P.M. to describe time. A.M. stands for the Latin words *ante meridiem.* It means before the Sun has crossed the meridian. P.M. stands for *post meridiem.* It means after the Sun has crossed the meridian. So 7:00 A.M. is in the morning, but 7:00 P.M. is in the evening.

16

Although the Sun will cross the meridian at 12:00 noon according to a sundial, it will not necessarily be noon according to your watch. This is a result of the way in which we set our clocks and watches. The clock time at which the Sun crosses the meridian will depend on your location and the time of **year.**

A sundial says 12:00 when the Sun reaches its highest point. A watch usually says something different.

Nowadays, we use the terms *A.M.* and *P.M.* to mean before and after 12:00 noon. They are no longer directly linked to the Sun's position in the sky.

The Sky at Night

At night, when the Sun is lighting up the other side of Earth, we can see some of the millions of other stars.

The constellations

On a clear night in the countryside, it is possible to look up and see about three thousand stars. On many nights, the Moon can be seen as well. In the past, sailors used the Moon and the stars to find their way at sea. Because Earth is spinning, the stars appear to move across the sky as the night goes on. Some form patterns that look like certain objects, animals, or people. In ancient times, people named them based on the shapes. Each pattern is called a **constellation.** The sky is divided into 88 constellations.

The Big Dipper, shown here, is part of the constellation called Ursa Major, or the Great Bear. It is easy to recognize.

The planets

In addition to the stars, we can sometimes see the **planets** Mercury, Venus, Mars, Jupiter, and Saturn. They are seen in different constellations as the **months** and the **years** go by. Occasionally, two or more planets appear close together in the sky.

Venus and Jupiter appear brighter than all the stars except the Sun. They can be seen here with Saturn and the Moon.

Seasonal Stars

From the **equator,** you can see all the stars at some point during the **year.** Most of them can be seen at some time during any particular night. Away from the equator, some stars can always be seen, some can be seen only sometimes, and some are never visible.

Circumpolar stars

The stars that can always be seen from a given position are called **circumpolar stars.** As Earth spins on its **axis,** the circumpolar stars in the **Northern Hemisphere** appear to rotate around the **North Star,** Polaris.

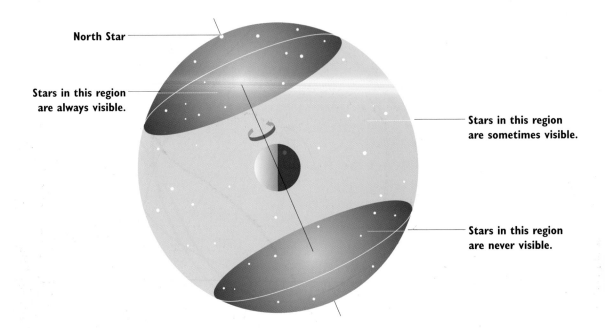

North Star

Stars in this region
are always visible.

Stars in this region
are sometimes visible.

Stars in this region
are never visible.

This diagram shows which stars can be seen from southern England, which is marked with a red dot. The same stars would be seen from other places in the world that are at the same distance from the North Pole.

Seeing Orion

The rest of the visible stars can be seen only at certain times. Like the Sun, they appear to rise and set. This is because of Earth's rotation. Each **day,** they rise and set about four minutes earlier than they did the day before. At times, they appear in the sky at the same time as the Sun. The **constellation** Orion, for example, is visible for only part of the year. At the other times, it appears in the sky during our **daytime.** The Sun is so bright during the day, we cannot see Orion or the other stars.

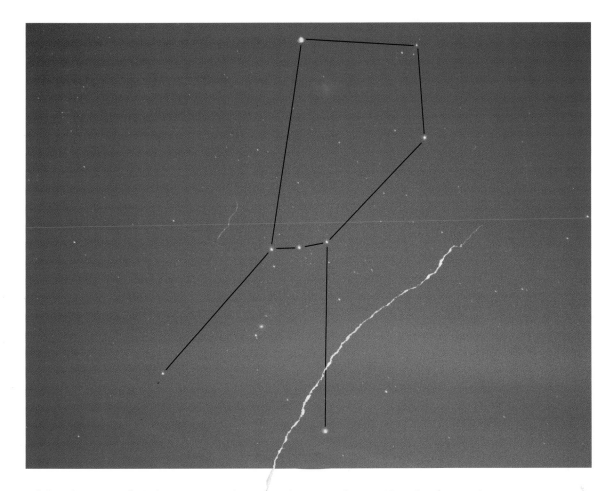

This picture of Orion was taken in the Northern Hemisphere. In the Southern Hemisphere, Orion looks a little bit different.

Our Moon

The Moon is our nearest neighbor in space. It is much smaller than Earth. In fact, Earth is about four times wider. The Moon is covered with craters that were formed when **meteoroids,** or lumps of rock in our **solar system,** made contact with it. Most were formed thousands of millions of **years** ago.

Things weigh less on the Moon

On the Moon, you would weigh less than you do on Earth. The force of **gravity** is less because the Moon is smaller. There is not enough gravity for the Moon to have an atmosphere around it.

The Moon rises and sets like the Sun. In this picture, it is about to set.

The surface of the Moon has many craters.

The far side of the Moon

The Moon turns on its **axis** once every 27.3 days. This is exactly the same rate that it **orbits** Earth. This is why the same side of the Moon always faces toward us. Nobody knew what the far side of the Moon looked like until 1959, when pictures were sent back to Earth by a Russian spacecraft. The United States is the only country to have landed people on the Moon. The first time was in July 1969. The sixth and last landing was in December 1972.

near side

far side

This model of the Moon was made before anyone knew what the far side of the Moon looked like.

Moon Phases

Reflecting light from the Sun

The Moon has no light of its own. We can see it only because it reflects light from the Sun. Half of the Moon always points toward the Sun, and half always points away. We are not always able to see the entire half that is facing the Sun. The amount of the lit face that can be seen changes as the Moon **orbits** Earth. You can see the different **phases of the Moon** in the diagram below.

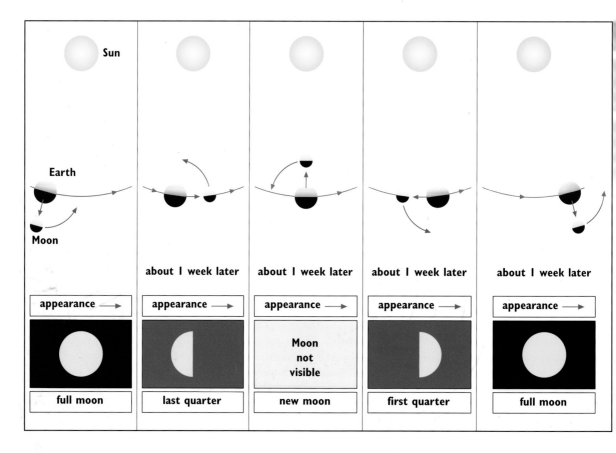

The Moon's appearance changes as it goes around its orbit.

New moon and full moon phases

When the Sun and the Moon are on opposite sides of Earth, the whole of the lit face can be seen. We call this a full moon. Roughly two weeks later, when the Moon passes between Earth and the Sun, none of the lit face can be seen. We call this a new moon.

The Moon from day to night

The Moon rises and sets about 50 minutes later from one **day** to the next. This means that on some nights, it will not be visible when it gets dark, but it may be visible when it gets light.

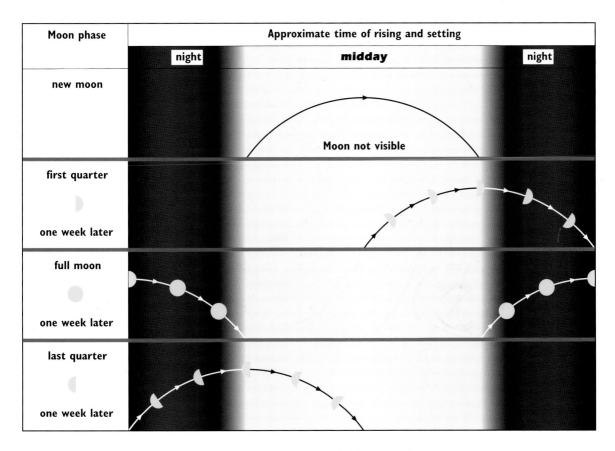

Different phases of the Moon are seen at different times of the day.

Eclipses

Eclipses of the Sun

The Moon goes around Earth. Every $29\frac{1}{2}$ **days,** it passes between Earth and the Sun, and there is a new moon. Normally, the Moon does not block the Sun from view when this happens. This is because its **orbit** is tilted. It passes unseen above or below the Sun in the sky.

A solar **eclipse** occurs if the Moon passes in front of the Sun and blocks part or all of it from view. During a total eclipse, the Moon completely blocks the Sun from view for a few seconds or minutes. When this happens, the **temperature** drops, and it gets dark enough for automatic street lights to come on.

Many people use special filters to observe solar eclipses. Never look directly at the Sun, even using sunglasses. It will damage your eyes.

Eclipses of the Moon

When there is a full moon, an eclipse of the Moon will sometimes occur. The Moon is on one side of Earth, and the Sun is on the other. Earth gets in the way, and prevents some of the Sun's light from falling on the Moon. In most eclipses of the Moon, part or all of the bright surface of the Moon gets very dark.

This is a partial eclipse of the Sun.

In this total eclipse of the Sun, the dark circle is the Moon.

Fact File

Not everyone calculates their **days** in the same way. Days in the Jewish and Muslim calendars begin at sunset rather than at midnight.

The last total **eclipse** of the Sun in the twentieth century occurred on August 11, 1999. It was visible from parts of Europe, the Middle East, and Asia.

When the Sun is very low in the sky, its shape appears to be oval rather than circular. This effect is caused by the bending of light by Earth's atmosphere.

It gets dark more suddenly after the Sun has set when you are closer to the **equator.**

The Moon can be seen at the time of the new moon only if there is an eclipse of the Sun.

Daylight saving time was first suggested by Benjamin Franklin in 1784. The idea was later promoted by William Willett in 1907. He suggested turning the clocks forward in four steps of twenty minutes for four weeks in a row.

In North America, daylight saving time generally starts on the first Sunday in April. It ends on the last Sunday in October. In the **Southern Hemisphere,** many countries follow daylight saving time from October to March.

If all the lights in a city were turned off, people there could see about ten times as many stars in the night sky.

Days and nights used to be shorter. The length of our day has increased by nearly 10 percent over the last 400 million years, as Earth's spin has slowed down.

As well as radiating light and energy, the Sun also throws particles out into space. When lots of particles arrive from the Sun at once, the night sky flickers with colored light. The effect is known as an aurora.

Glossary

A.M. originally used to mean a time in the morning before the Sun had crossed the meridian. Today, it is used to mean a time in the morning before 12:00 noon.

axis imaginary line passing through the center of a planet from the North to the South Pole, around which the planet spins

circumpolar star star that travels around a pole and is always visible in that hemisphere in a clear night sky

clockwise direction in which the hands of a clock move

constellation group of stars in the night sky

counterclockwise opposite direction to the way in which the hands on a clock move

day length of time based on the time it takes for Earth to spin around once on its axis

daylight saving time time system used in some countries during the summer months. It is normally one hour ahead of the time used during the winter months.

daytime time between sunrise and sunset

eclipse one heavenly body blocking all or part of another from view.

energy what it takes to heat something up or to make it move

equator imaginary line that separates Earth's Northern and Southern Hemispheres

galaxy group of stars (usually a billion or more) on its own in space

gnomon part of a sundial that casts the shadow

gravity force that attracts objects to each other. Earth's gravity gives us our weight.

horizon line where the sky appears to meet the land

local time time system that uses the actual position of the Sun in the sky

meridian line that runs in a north-south direction, and if extended, would pass through Earth's North and South Poles

meteoroid rocklike object that travels through space

midday time when the Sun reaches its highest point of the day (and crosses the meridian)

month length of time based on the time it takes for the Moon to orbit Earth once

nighttime time between sunset and sunrise

30

Northern Hemisphere half of Earth north of the equator; the top half of a globe

North Star star situated directly above Earth's North Pole; the only star that does not appear to move as Earth spins on its axis

orbit path of a planet around the Sun, or of a moon around a planet

phase of the Moon shape of the lit portion of the Moon as seen from Earth

planet object in the shape of a ball that orbits the Sun

P.M. originally used to mean a time in the afternoon or evening after the Sun had crossed the meridian. Today, it is used to mean a time in the afternoon or evening after 12:00 noon.

radiate to send out energy in waves or rays

solar system Sun and the planets (like Earth) that orbit it

Southern Hemisphere half of Earth south of the equator; the bottom half of a globe

sundial device that uses shadows to find the time from the Sun's position in the sky

temperature how hot or cold something is

time zone part of Earth in which everyone sets their clocks and watches to the same time

year length of time based on the time taken for Earth to orbit the Sun and for the cycle of seasons to repeat itself. A normal calendar year has 365 days. A leap year has 366 days.

More Books to Read

Aronson, Billy. *Eclipses: Nature's Blackouts.* Danbury, Conn.: Franklin Watts Inc., 1997.

Gardner, Robert. *Science Project Ideas About the Moon.* Berkeley Heights, N.J.: Enslow Publishers, Inc., 1997.

Gardner, Robert. *Science Project Ideas About the Sun.* Berkeley Heights, N.J.: Enslow Publishers, Inc., 1997.

Index